SOCCER

RULES, TIPS, STRATEGY, AND SAFETY

BRIAN WINGATE

New York

To Oliver

Published in 2007 by The Rosen Publishing Group, Inc.
29 East 21st Street, New York, NY 10010

First Edition

Library of Congress Cataloging-in-Publication Data

Wingate, Brian.
Soccer: rules, tips, strategy, and safety/Brian Wingate.—1st ed.
p. cm.—(Sports from coast to coast)
Includes bibliographical references and index.
ISBN-13: 978-1-4042-0995-4
ISBN-10: 1-4042-0995-6 (library binding)
1. Soccer—Juvenile literature. I. Title. II. Series.
GV943.25.W57 2007
796.334—dc22

2006014274

Manufactured in the United States of America

CONTENTS

CHAPTER ONE

A Timeless Game

An athlete balances a ball on his knee in this relief carving from ancient Greece. This image is reproduced on the European Cup soccer trophy.

Playing soccer, it seems, is a part of human nature. There are accounts throughout history and from all over the world of people playing games in which they move a ball across a playing field toward a goal at the other end. In Mexico, the Mayans played their own version of a kicking game, called Pok-A-Tok, as early as 3000 BC. Archaeologists have unearthed a playing field that is more than 3,500 years old! Historical records also show the Chinese played a game similar to soccer for their emperor's birthday celebration about 2500 BC. They called the game Tsu Chu, meaning "to kick a stuffed leather ball."

Around 2000 BC., the Greeks played a game called Episkyros with a ball made from inflated pig bladders. Earlier models were constructed of linen and hair wrapped tightly in string and then sewn together. The Romans created their own version of the game, Harpastum, which used a smaller ball and was played more like rugby than soccer.

Blood Sport

In the eighth century, people in Britain took part in mob football, in which entire villages played against each other. These matches were so violent that many hid in their homes and shuttered the windows. The origins of mob football are unclear, but one story tells of the severed head of a defeated prince being used as the ball.

Over the centuries, attempts were made to keep the sport from becoming too violent. Britain's King Edward II was so disturbed that he banned mob football in 1314. His ban was unsuccessful, and for the next four centuries, rulers throughout Europe tried to keep their subjects from playing the sport. In France, Kings Philippe V and Charles V both tried to outlaw the violent game. During the fifteenth century, Scottish kings James I and James II tried to keep football out of their country. In 1540, King Henry VIII of England outlawed football, even though there is evidence that he played the sport himself. Finally, in 1681, football gained royal approval when King Charles II of England publicly attended a match.

Laying Down the Laws

In 1815, Eton College in England established a set of rules that other teams began to follow. In 1848, these rules were officially adopted and named the

In this painting by Giorgio Vasari (1511–1574), townspeople in Florence, Italy, flock to the town square to watch a soccer-type game called *calcio*.

Cambridge Rules. This marked a crossroads for the sport, which was called football at the time. Players in Britain soon divided into two camps. One side supported the Cambridge Rules and the attempt to reduce violence in the sport. (Under the new rules, tripping and "hacking," or shin kicking, were prohibited.) The other side preferred rules followed by the Rugby School, which allowed for rougher play.

In 1863, the London Football Association settled the dispute and split the sport in two. There was rugby football, which kept many of the old

Soccer or Football?

The term "soccer" came about in the 1880s at Oxford University, in Great Britain. A slang term for rugby was "rugger." A player named Charles Wreford Brown took the middle of the word "association" football, added an "er," and coined the term "soccer." In North America, the term stuck. However, most fans around the world (including those in Britain) still refer to their beloved sport as football.

rules. Then there was association football, which became soccer as we know it today.

Refining the rules fueled the popularity of soccer in Britain. Amateur soccer clubs sprouted up everywhere, and the first annual tournament was established in 1871. The following year, England and Scotland met in the first international match.

Here Comes FIFA

Soccer spread around the globe, and it soon became clear that there was a need for international rules. In 1904, seven European soccer associations founded the Federation Internationale de Football Association, or FIFA. FIFA was designed to oversee soccer operations throughout the world and encourage a high level of competition.

FIFA certainly achieved its goals. In 1930, the first World Cup tournament was held in Uruguay, South America, to determine the best team in soccer. Uruguay took advantage of the home field and won the World Cup that year. The United States finished fourth in the competition, the best finish for the men's team in the tournament so far. Since 1930, the World Cup has only risen in popularity. In 2004, FIFA boasted more member countries (204)

Pelé Comes to America

A huge part of soccer's growth in the United States came from a big Brazilian star with a short name: Pelé. Born Edson Arantes do Nascimento, Pelé is considered by many to be the best player in the history of the sport. He became a worldwide star when he led Brazil to three World Cup trophies from 1958 to 1970. He retired in 1974.

At the time, professional soccer had been struggling to find an audience in North America. Then, in 1975, the New York Cosmos of the North American Soccer League (NASL) persuaded Pelé to come out of retirement and play for them. Electrifying audiences for three more years, Pelé and his presence on the American soccer scene put the sport in the spotlight. Thousands of kids across the United States picked up this sport, which was easy and fun to play, and required little equipment. The NASL closed at the end of the 1984 season, after showcasing the fun of soccer for nearly twenty years.

Pelé scans the field for defenders as he dribbles downfield with the ball during a game for the New York Cosmos.

In 1930, fans packed the stands in Uruguay's Centenario Stadium for the first World Cup championship match. Uruguay won the game by a score of 4–2.

than the United Nations. The level of competition for the World Cup championship is fierce, and passions run high. The tournament is held every four years, and only the top thirty-two teams in the world are invited to compete for the Cup.

Women's Soccer Makes a Splash

In the 1990s, it was time for America's women soccer players to take the world stage. First, in 1991, the U.S. women's team won the FIFA World Cup

Players on the U.S. women's soccer team raise the championship trophy following their victory in the 1999 FIFA World Cup final. It was the U.S. women's second World Cup championship.

tournament held in China. It was the first World Cup championship for any American team. Four years later, they made another strong World Cup showing, coming in third in the tournament held in Sweden. When the United States hosted the 1999 World Cup, more than three million fans attended the tournament games. Millions more worldwide watched the action on television. With a strong team led by superstar Mia Hamm, the American women's team won the World Cup final, beating the Chinese women's team in a shoot-out.

Into the New Millennium

In exchange for hosting the men's World Cup in 1994, the United States Soccer Federation founded Major League Soccer (MLS) in 1996. More than ten years later, Major League Soccer is well established, although it has not yet generated the same level of fan support as basketball, football, and baseball in the United States. Hockey, Canada's national sport, still dominates the headlines up north. But youth leagues are popular all over North America, and every year more people discover the fun of the "world's game."

CHAPTER TWO

Getting on the Field

Soccer is a fast-growing sport in the United States, especially among female players.

According to the United States Soccer Federation, more than eighteen million Americans play soccer. And the number is on the rise. The Sporting Goods Manufacturing Association claims that high school soccer participation almost doubled, increasing 88 percent, between 1990 and 2004. Many schools have their own soccer fields, where students play during the week. On the weekends, these same fields often play host to popular local league games.

The Goal

A rectangular goal, usually a frame made of metal, sits in the middle of each goal line. Goal posts and cross-bars must be white. A regulation goal is 8 feet (2.4 meters) tall and 8 yards (7.3 m) wide. A net is attached to the frame to catch any balls that get past the goalkeeper, or goalie, the player who guards the goal. The net extends about 6 feet (1.8 m) behind the goal.

The Field

Ideally, the entire playing surface of a soccer field—also called a pitch—is covered by short-cut grass. The field may vary in size, depending on the league, but it must be a rectangle. The two halves of the field are separated

Compared to the size of a soccer ball, the goal looks gigantic. But scoring a goal is not as easy as it looks. Shooters must practice placing kicks precisely in the corners of the goal, out of the goalkeeper's reach.

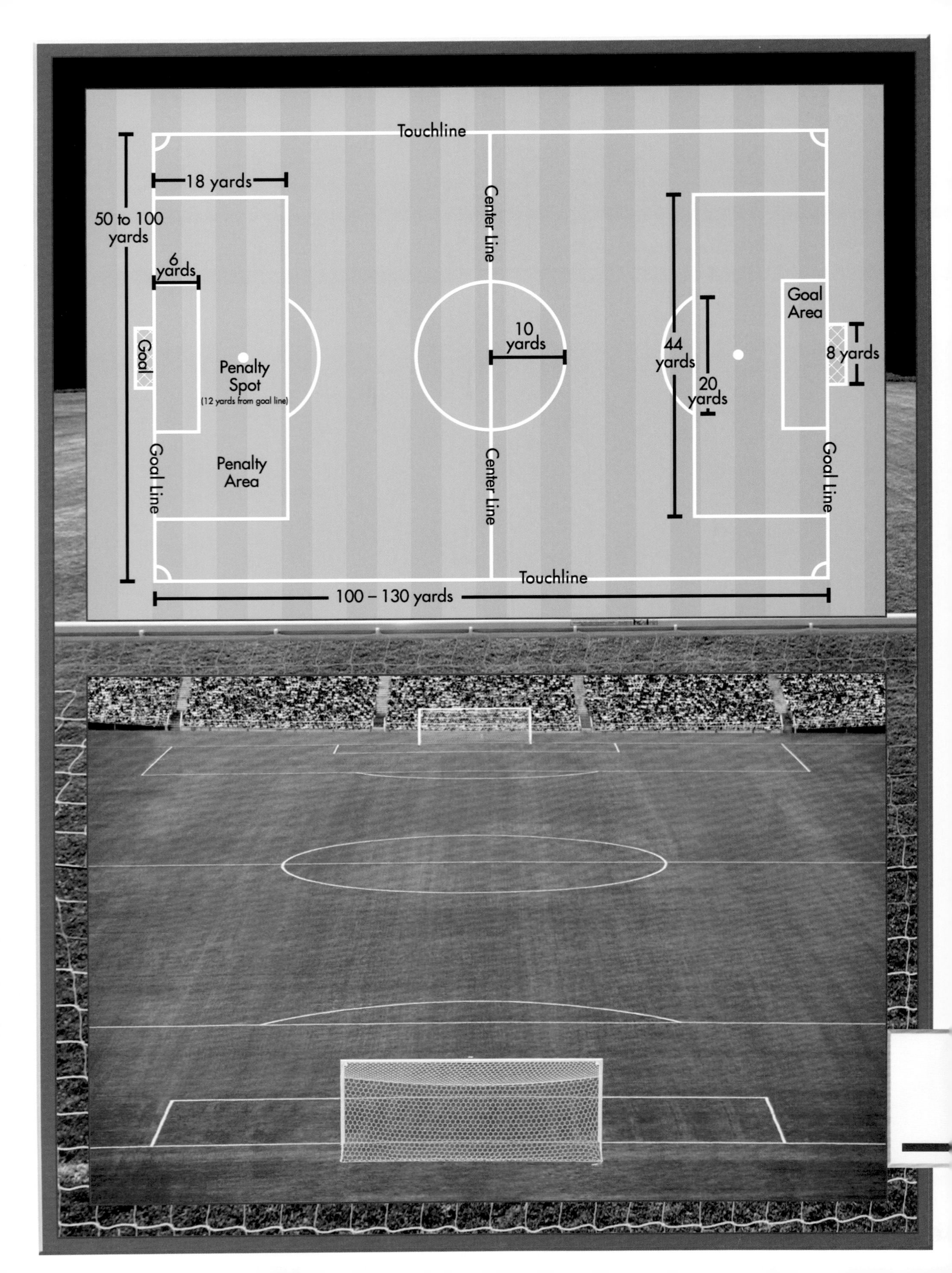
Touchline
18 yards
50 to 100 yards
6 yards
Goal
Penalty Spot
(12 yards from goal line)
Goal Line
Penalty Area
Center Line
10 yards
Center Line
44 yards
20 yards
Goal Area
8 yards
Goal Line
Touchline
100 – 130 yards

by the center line. In the middle of this line is a circle with a 10-yard (9.1 m) radius. The ball is placed in the center of this circle at the beginning of both halves of the match and after goals, to restart play.

The area in front of the goal is marked with two rectangles. The smaller one is the goal area, and the larger one is the penalty area. The goalie (and only the goalie) may handle the ball in the penalty area.

A flag marks each corner of a soccer field. A quarter-circle is drawn within the field, one yard from the flag post. Special kicks called corner kicks are made with the ball placed within these quarter-circles.

The Ball

Most leagues use balls made of leather or similar materials that have been approved by FIFA. Balls come in several sizes. Upper levels use a ball that is approximately 27 to 28 inches (69–71 centimeters) in circumference and weighs about one pound. Youth leagues often use a smaller, lighter ball.

The Players

The maximum number of players on a team varies depending on the level. Professional teams usually have a total of about fourteen players. At game time, each team has eleven players on the field. The rest wait until one of their teammates needs a break. World Cup rules allow a maximum of three substitutions per match, so team sizes are kept relatively small. Youth leagues that allow unlimited substitutions may have twenty players or more.

To be approved by FIFA for international play, a field must be between 100 and 130 yards long (90–120 m) and 50 to 100 yards wide (45–90 m). The shorter lines at the end of the field are the goal lines. The longer lines along the sides are touchlines. When the entire soccer ball crosses one of these lines, it is considered out of play.

After making a save, the goalie may begin a counterattack by quickly rolling the ball to a teammate headed up the field.

The Positions

Most teams use some variation of the following basic player positions. Each player has a certain zone or area of the field that he or she patrols.

Goalie

In some ways the goalie is the most important player on the field. It's the goalie's job to protect the goal and keep the other team from scoring. The goalie (also called a goalkeeper or keeper) can use any part of the body to protect the goal while he or she is in the penalty box area. A good goalkeeper is calm under pressure and is not afraid to jump in the way of a speeding ball. As an attacking player approaches with the ball, the keeper stands in a slight crouch, ready to spring in any direction. The keeper may suddenly charge toward the oncoming player, reducing the chance for a good shot on goal. During a corner kick, the keeper will often lunge into the air and knock the ball away with a closed fist. The ability to use his or her hands helps the goalie rise above the crowd and reach the ball first. Once out of the penalty area, however, the keeper is treated like any other player and may not use his or her hands. For this reason, keepers rarely venture out of the penalty area unless the ball is deep in the opponent's territory.

Defenders

A player jumps to control the ball as his opponent closes in to defend.

Three or four players remain near their own goal area to defend their side of the field. Center-backs and fullbacks serve as the goalkeeper's last line of protection. When the opposing team tries to score, these backs try to take the ball away by disrupting the play. Most teams use four defensive players and employ one of two styles of defense: zone or man-to-man. There are many variations within these two styles. In a zone defense, each player defends a certain area of the field. In man-to-man, each defender covers, or marks, an offensive player closely, trying to prevent him or her from getting the ball. The sweeper, a type of center-back, is often the cornerstone of the defensive unit. The sweeper is usually the player closest to the goalie, and it is his or her job to "sweep" out any ball that gets past the other defenders.

The goalkeeper and the defenders work together closely to form a tight defense. The goalie may call out suggestions or alert a defender to an oncoming player. If a defender gains possession of the ball, he or she may pass it back to the keeper. In the past, the keeper could pick up a backward pass with his or her hands. But some players and fans felt that keepers held the ball too long. The rules were changed to speed up the game, and now the keeper must clear a backward pass with a kick.

Two opposing players race to the ball near midfield. The player in the striped jersey effectively uses his upper body to block his opponent's access to the ball.

Midfielders

Midfield players often help out both defensive and offensive teammates in a pinch. Also called halfbacks, midfielders serve as the first line of defense against the attacking team. In addition, midfielders set up offensive attacks with crisp passes to the front lines. Teams often use three midfielders: one in the middle and one on each side of the field. Well-rounded players with a knack for the passing game make great midfielders.

Attackers

Attacking players are offensive specialists who stay on the front lines and try to score. Teams usually spread three or four attackers across the field to make themselves difficult to defend. One or two center forwards (called strikers) anchor the middle of the field, while wing players attack from the sides. The striker is a team's main offensive threat. During play, the striker is most often found near the opponent's goal, covered closely by the defense. When receiving a pass, the striker must be able to control the ball quickly, evade defensive pressure, and unleash a shot on goal.

An attacker speeds toward the keeper with no defenders in sight. Clean breakaways like this are rare in soccer.

Equipment

Compared to a sport like U.S. football, soccer requires very little equipment. But each piece serves an important purpose. Here's a look at soccer equipment from the ground up.

Footwear

Since feet do most of the work in soccer, it makes sense that they have the most equipment. Players must wear cleats, shin guards, and socks to protect their feet and legs. Cleats are the shoes that every player must wear. The bottoms of the shoes are covered with small cleats, or knobs, that provide

Soccer = *Foot*ball

The foot is a valuable tool in soccer. Each part of the foot is best used for a specific purpose.

Instep Controlling the ball, dribbling, and passing.

Outside Turning, dribbling, and passing the ball to the side.

Top (shoelaces) Best for kicking and shooting.

Heel Use sparingly for quick backward passes.

Sole (bottom) Use sparingly for trapping or trick moves.

Toes Least amount of ball control. Try to avoid using your toes.

traction in all playing conditions. Most cleats have hard rubber soles and a leather upper.

Shin guards are the only piece of required safety gear. They cover the front of the leg from the ankle to just below the knee. Some shin guards are made of hard, molded-plastic strips inserted into a stiff cloth backing to protect the leg. Other models are designed with a single piece of hard plastic formed around a backing of foam. Extra-long socks keep the shin guards in place.

Shorts and Shirts

Team members wear jerseys of the same color. (Goalies, however, wear a different-colored jersey for easier identification.) Each team in a league has a different color jersey. Every player has his or her own number displayed prominently on the back of the shirt.

Soccer shorts are made of lightweight material like nylon. Heavy fabrics would restrict leg movement and absorb sweat, two things that would only slow a player down.

Goalie Goods

The goalkeeper must be prepared to dive to the ground at any time to defend against a shot. For this reason, goalies often wear long-sleeved shirts with

Goalies can cover much of the net with proper positioning and by jumping with their arms and legs spread.

padding in the elbows. Long shorts with padding along the hips are also common. In addition, many goalies choose to wear padded gloves that protect their hands and provide a better grip on the ball.

Coaches

Most soccer teams have one or two coaches who guide the players throughout the season. A coach helps a player in all areas of his or her game. For practices, coaches design and conduct drills and exercises that will help players improve their ball control, shot placement, and game-time decision-making. The coach also assigns the position of each player, determines game strategy, and decides when to substitute in fresh players.

CHAPTER THREE

Start the Action

When the starting whistle blows, all of a player's skills are put to the test. This attacker uses the outside of his foot to dribble downfield.

The sun is shining, and the field is marked. The players are dressed for the game and have discussed their game strategy with the coaches. The referee blows a whistle, letting everyone know that it's time to begin.

Let the Game Begin

Every soccer game begins with a coin toss at the center of the field. The team that wins the toss either gets the ball first or chooses which side of the field to defend in the first half.

Once the sides have been determined, each team assembles eleven players on the field. The ball is placed directly on the center line in the middle of the field. Usually, two players from the team receiving the ball first line up behind the ball. The opposing team must wait on the outside of the center circle.

An official blows the whistle to signal the start of the game, and the center forward kicks the ball. The ball must travel forward one complete rotation before it is officially in play. The player who does the kickoff may not touch the ball again until another player has touched it.

Both teams try to control the ball. Any player may strike it using any part of his or her body except the hands and arms. The ball remains in play until a foul is committed or it goes out of bounds.

Corner and Goal Kicks

If the ball goes out of bounds over one of the goal lines, play is resumed with either a corner kick or a goal kick. A corner kick occurs when the defending team last touches the ball. The attacking team places the ball in the quarter-circle at the corner of the field and kicks the ball back into play. Most teams design special plays for corner kicks. Players might rush in from outside the penalty area just as the ball is kicked from the corner. Good players precisely aim corner kicks to one of these teammates who can "one-touch" the ball into the goal with a well-placed kick or header.

When the attacking team kicks the ball out of bounds over the goal line, the defending team places the ball in the goal area for a goal kick. All opposing players must vacate the penalty area. The goalie or a fullback then kicks the ball to resume play. The ball is not officially in play again until it leaves the penalty area. Some teams prefer to make short goal kicks to a midfield player nearby, while others try to kick the ball way downfield to a waiting forward.

The referee looks on as a corner kick sails toward the goal. A common strategy is to kick the ball to the front of the goal, where a teammate can knock it home.

Time Is Ticking

According to FIFA rules, every soccer game is ninety minutes long, divided into two forty-five-minute halves. Players get a fifteen-minute break before the second half. Since field conditions may vary, the teams switch sides of the field at the start of the second half. Most youth leagues play shorter games to accommodate the fitness level of young athletes. Players between twelve and thirteen years old play two thirty-five-minute halves, while fourteen- and fifteen-year-olds typically play two forty-minute halves.

The Throw-In

If the ball fully crosses a touchline, it is declared out of bounds, and the game is stopped. The team that last touched the ball loses possession, and a player from the opposing team performs a throw-in. For a regulation throw-in:

1. Locate the point where the ball went out of bounds; this will be the spot for the throw-in. Face the field. Place one hand on each side of the ball and raise the ball above your head.

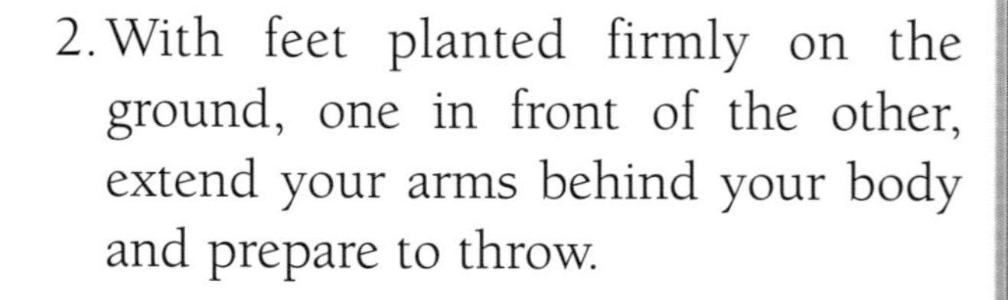

2. With feet planted firmly on the ground, one in front of the other, extend your arms behind your body and prepare to throw.

3. Bring the ball forward and release with both hands at the same time. Keep both feet in contact with the ground as you release the ball. Be sure not to step into the field of play.

Tip: For added power, take a running start before the throw-in. Be sure to throw at the appropriate spot and keep both feet on the ground. Plant your front foot and drag the back foot forward as you release the ball. This helps you throw the ball farther using the power generated by your torso.

This player is properly dragging his back foot as he throws in. Both feet must be in contact with the ground at the moment the ball is released.

If a game is tied at the end of regulation, extra time may be needed to determine the winner. In some cases, the winner is determined by a tiebreaker or shoot-out. Each team gets five free kicks from the penalty spot, and the keeper tries to stop the shots. The team with more goals after five shots wins the game. If both teams score the same number of goals, the shoot-out continues until one team scores and the other does not.

Referees and Penalties

The referee patrols the field and makes sure that everyone is playing by the rules. In professional soccer leagues, two assistants join the referee. They determine who kicked the ball out of bounds, and they use hand signals to communicate stoppages of play.

When a referee spots a player breaking the rules, he may stop play and hold out a yellow card above the player. This serves as a warning to the player to stop the behavior. If the player commits another foul, he or she will receive a red card and be ejected from the game. Some actions, like abusive language, fighting, or violent play, can result in an automatic red card and suspension. The team is not allowed to substitute for the ejected player and must play shorthanded for the remainder of the game.

Yellow cards and red cards are reserved for the more serious fouls committed during a game. The referee stops play for other fouls as well. Play is resumed with a free kick by the team that did not commit the penalty. There are several types of free kicks:

- **Indirect.** Less serious offenses result in an indirect kick to resume play. The kick occurs at the site of the foul. It is not possible to score a goal on an indirect kick. The ball must first touch another player.
- **Direct.** A direct kick is reserved for serious fouls, like touching the ball with your hands or violent play. A goal may be scored from a direct kick. Opposing players must stand at least ten yards away when the ball is kicked. If a direct kick is near the goal, defensive

A frustrated player throws up her hands as the referee holds up a red card, ejecting her from the game. Once a red card is issued, it will not be reversed.

players may group themselves together ten yards away to form a defensive "wall." This obstructs the kicker's view and reduces the chances of a goal being scored.

- **Penalty.** If a defensive player commits a serious foul in his or her own penalty area, a penalty kick is awarded to the opposing team. The ball is placed on the penalty spot, and one player is allowed to take a shot on goal. All players except the shooter and the goalie must clear out of the penalty area until the ball is kicked. It is very

An assistant referee *(above)* watches closely for an offsides violation. A flag is raised to indicate where the violation occurred.

difficult for a goalie to stop a penalty shot. Professional goalies try to anticipate where the ball will be kicked so they can move into position. This can be difficult because skilled kickers disguise the direction of their shot until the last moment. If the goalie moves too soon, the kicker can kick the other way.

Offsides

The rule in soccer that creates the most confusion is the Offsides Law. The penalty is intended to prevent offensive players from hanging around the opponent's goal, waiting to score. The rule states that at least two defensive players (including the keeper) must be between an offensive player and the goal when the ball is passed in the offensive player's direction. This essentially means that an offensive player must stay even with the defender closest to the goal before receiving a pass from a teammate.

Essential Skills

There are six essential skills that every aspiring soccer player should develop. These skills must be practiced over and over before one can become a top-notch player. There is no such thing as the "perfect player," so there is always a part of your game that you can improve.

Dribbling

Dribbling is the art of running and changing direction while controlling the ball with your feet. In the beginning, you want to get used to the feel of running quickly while propelling the ball a short distance in front of you with light kicks. As you gain confidence, you'll learn to change direction and evade defenders. To dribble past an opponent, slow down as you approach. Then, just as you reach the opponent, pass by with a sudden burst of speed and change of direction.

Keeping your head up while dribbling allows you to stay aware of the positions and movements of all the players on the field.

Try to keep the ball moving at all times. A stopped ball is more likely to be taken away by a defender. Keep your head up so you can keep an eye on the field around you. If you have to stop dribbling, keep possession of the ball by turning your back and using your body to block your opponent. Be careful not to push or hold the opposing player with your arms, which is a foul.

Passing

Accurate passing is often the secret of a team's offensive success. For a short pass, kick the ball with the inside (instep) of your foot. The instep is the

The pass arrives just in time for this player to control the ball without breaking stride.

largest kicking surface and gives you the greatest accuracy. For a long pass downfield, kick with the top of your foot along the shoelaces to loft the ball through the air. The outside of your foot is great for quick passes to the side. It is important to practice passing with both feet.

There are several passing strategies that can quickly penetrate the defense of an opposing team. One of the most common is the wall pass. When a defender approaches as you are dribbling the ball, pass the ball to a teammate slightly ahead of you and to the side. As the defender shifts to cover your teammate, sprint hard down the field. Your teammate can then pass the ball back to you. Your teammate serves as the "wall" that bounces your pass right back to you.

Shooting

Scoring opportunities are worthless unless they are converted into goals. Mastering the art of shooting with both feet takes practice and patience. As you practice your passing game, you are actually building all the skills necessary to be a great shooter: ball control, accurate ball placement, and power.

Good players can make the ball spin or curve in the air by striking it on certain spots and with different parts of their foot. When shooting, keep your arms out for balance, and keep your head over the ball. This helps the ball stay low and improves your accuracy. When you're trying to score, aim at the far corners of the net.

Trapping

Trapping is an important part of ball control. When a teammate passes you the ball, you have to settle the ball to the ground quickly. This often requires you to "trap" the ball with some part of your body so that it doesn't bounce out of control. Effective trapping is possible with virtually any part of the body. Experienced players can trap the ball with their legs, chest, feet, and even their backside.

To trap the ball, you must use your body to absorb the speed of the ball. As the ball reaches your foot or chest, let your body relax. If your body is tense, the ball will bounce too far from you to control.

For a chest trap, this player collapses his chest to absorb the impact of the ball. This allows him to bring the ball softly to the ground.

Tackling

Attacking the player with the ball—tackling—is an important skill. You may knock the ball away from the front, back, or side as your opponent dribbles it. Some players even dive and slide to knock the ball away. A referee will call a foul if it appears that you were not pursuing the ball and instead used your body to knock the other player down or off

This defender executes a perfect slide tackle to knock the ball away. A slide tackle is always a risky choice: An attacker who avoids the tackle may be several yards past you before you can even get off the ground.

balance. Especially when attempting a slide tackle, make sure that you touch the ball before making contact with any part of your opponent's body. If you strike your opponent's body first, you will be called for a foul.

Headers

In soccer, your head is another tool you can use for controlling the ball. With practice, you can turn your head just as you make contact with the ball, sending it in any direction you want. A simple practice drill can improve your

A header can be a dangerous scoring weapon in the goal area. In a game dominated by kicking skills, a header can quickly change the direction of the ball and surprise the keeper who is not expecting it.

headers. Stand a few feet from a teammate and have him or her gently throw the ball in the air toward you. Return the ball by striking it with your forehead. Your teammate can move to the side or stand farther back to help you expand your header skills.

CHAPTER FOUR

Doing It Yourself

Soccer players must be in fantastic shape to play the game at a high level. In the early weeks of a season, it is common to see players with their hands on their knees, trying to catch their breath.

Staying in Shape

It helps to get your body in gear before the season begins. There are many fun ways to train the muscles that you will use in a soccer game. Riding a bike is great for building strong legs and endurance. Swimming provides a full-body workout and improves lung capacity. You're on the right track if you're exercising your body at least three times per week.

It is very important that your muscles and bones have the right fuel to power you through

Players stretch their hamstrings (the largest muscles in the back of the leg) prior to playing soccer. Flexibility is essential for such a physically demanding sport.

the soccer season. Be sure to eat a balanced diet. Try to avoid processed foods such as candy and soda. The high sugar content doesn't give your body the consistent energy it needs. Complex carbohydrates, like pasta, are a great choice for dinner the night before a game. Breads and pastas are easily broken down by your muscles into usable energy. Get to bed early, too. While you sleep, your body repairs itself and gets ready for the next big game.

Warming Up, Cooling Down

Once the whistle blows to start the game, you can go from a standstill to a full run in a matter of seconds. If your muscles aren't ready, you have a much higher risk of injury. Before a game, players usually warm up their bodies with light running, stretching, and some passing and shooting drills. Take this time seriously, and be sure you stretch before you step onto the field.

If you have time for only a few stretches, be sure you warm up all the major muscle groups in your legs. Quadriceps are the powerful muscles that run from your knees to your hip and provide your kicking and acceleration power. Your hamstrings cover the back side of your upper leg and must be stretched to

Drink plenty of fluids before, during, and after every game.

Leg Stretches

- **Quadriceps:** Stand upright on both feet. Bend one leg behind you, raising your foot to your buttock. Using the hand on the same side of your body, gently pull your foot closer to the buttock. Feel the stretch in the front of your leg.

- **Hamstrings:** Stand upright on both feet. Keeping your back straight, slowly bend forward and let your arms dangle. You will feel a stretch in the back of your legs. Don't bounce.

- **Calves:** Stand with both feet on a stair or another slightly elevated surface. Place the toes of one foot on the edge of the stair and slowly let your body weight extend your heel downward. You will feel a stretch in the calf muscles.

maintain balance between muscle groups. Your calf muscles run from the heel to the back of the knee and help push off from the ground when running.

When the game ends, be sure to give your body some time to cool down before you stop moving. Walk slowly around the field until your heart rate returns to normal. Cool down and drink plenty of fluids, and your body will not be as sore the following day.

Injuries

By warming up and cooling down faithfully, you may be able to avoid one of soccer's most common injuries—the muscle cramp. A muscle cramp happens when one or more muscles contract powerfully and stay that way. Cramps can be quite painful. It usually helps to gently stretch out the muscle that is cramping. The good news about cramps is that they don't last long.

Many rules in soccer are designed to avoid injuries. For instance, players are not allowed to kick the ball near another player's head. Also, sliding into an opponent's legs is forbidden. These rules help maintain the safety of the sport. But with every sport, injuries do occur. The most vulnerable parts of the soccer athlete's body are the knees and ankles. The legs take a lot of abuse in a full-speed game of soccer. The ligaments and tendons that hold your knees and ankles together can be stretched if you fall or twist in an awkward way. If you have injured yourself in the past, it is always wise to use extra protection during games. You can purchase a soft brace to stabilize a weakened knee or ankle.

Buying Equipment

Once you've decided you want to play soccer, it doesn't take much equipment to get started. A ball is all that's really needed to play with friends in your neighborhood. When joining a team, you'll need to buy cleats, socks, shorts, and shin guards. You can usually find all these things at your local sporting goods store. Cleats are the most expensive item and, in many ways, the most important. Take your time when selecting cleats. If you wear two pairs of socks in a game, don't forget to wear two pairs to the shoe store. A shoe that fits just right with one pair of socks will be too tight with two. Most teams supply the official jersey for you to wear, so don't worry about buying one.

Youth Leagues

Getting started on a team is pretty easy. Soccer is one of the most popular sports for young people, and there are youth leagues throughout North America. Several large organizations oversee league activities. There are also many local independent leagues to choose from. Most leagues have teams for players from the ages of five to eighteen. Both boys and girls are invited to

Soccer camps give young players an opportunity to learn skills from some of the sport's best. Here, soccer superstar Mia Hamm works with a group of girls at a soccer camp in Los Angeles, California.

play. Some leagues mix boys and girls together on the same teams (called "coed" teams), while others maintain a separate league for each.

A soccer season usually lasts about three months. Many leagues organize one season in the spring and another in the fall. A common spring schedule is March through May, and a fall season may run from September through November. During the season, you will probably practice with your team once during the week and then play a game on Saturday. Be prepared for a range of temperatures. A spring season that starts with frosty grass in March can end with scorching sun in late May.

Soccer camps are a great way to improve your skills and stay in shape during the summer months. It's fun to meet other players, too. Camps usually last one or two weeks. Experienced instructors spend hours each day honing every aspect of your game.

Many high schools assemble their own soccer teams to compete against other school teams. Coaches hold tryouts at a certain time of the year to select the best players. Those who are exceptionally skilled may go on to play competitive soccer at the college level or even the professional level. For the rest of us, colleges and universities generally have intramural programs, which are mini-leagues that are open to all students. There are opportunities to play team soccer well into your adult life, as municipal adult leagues are common in most areas.

Winning Isn't Everything

Soccer, like any sport, can be highly competitive. Some athletes dedicate their lives to it and want to win at all costs. But the majority of athletes just play for the love of the game. If you enjoy soccer but don't expect to be the next David Beckham or Ronaldinho, don't worry. The key is to have fun.

GLOSSARY

center forward A player who is positioned in the middle of the field on offense.

cleats Sports shoes that have hard rubber spikes attached to the underside to provide traction.

corner kick A direct free kick from a corner of the field. It is awarded to the attacking team when the ball has been driven out of bounds over the goal line by a defender.

fullback A primarily defensive backfield player whose position is near the defensive goal.

goal kick A free kick that is awarded to a defensive team when an opponent has driven the ball out of bounds over the goal line.

halfback One of several players stationed behind the forward line of attacking players.

instep The arched middle part of the foot between the toes and the ankle.

offsides Illegally ahead of the ball in the attacking zone.

throw-in A way to restart play after the ball has gone out of bounds.

touchline Either of the sidelines bordering the playing field.

wing Either of the forward positions played near the sideline.

FOR MORE INFORMATION

American Youth Soccer Organization
12501 S. Isis Avenue
Hawthorne, CA 90250
(800) 872-2976
Web site: http://www.soccer.org

National Soccer Hall of Fame
18 Stadium Circle
Oneonta, NY 13820
(607) 432-3351
Web site: http://www.soccerhall.org

U.S. Amateur Soccer Association
9152 Kent Avenue, Suite C-50
Lawrence, IN 46216
(317) 541-8564
Web site: http://www.usasa.com

U.S. Soccer Association
1801 S. Prairie Avenue
Chicago, IL 60616
(312) 808-1300
Web site: http://www.ussoccer.com

U.S. Youth Soccer Association
899 Presidential Drive, Suite 117
Richardson, TX 75081
(972) 235-4499
Web site: http://www.usyouthsoccer.org

Web Sites

Due to the changing nature of Internet links, Rosen Publishing has developed an online list of Web sites related to the subject of this book. This site is updated regularly. Please use this link to access the list:

http://www.rosenlinks.com/scc/socc

FOR FURTHER READING

Baddiel, Ivor. *Soccer: The Ultimate World Cup Companion*. New York, NY: DK Publishing, 1998.

Garland, Jim. *Youth Soccer Drills: 77 Drills for Beginning to Intermediate Players*. Champaign, IL: Human Kinetics, 1997.

Lover, Stanley. *Soccer Rules Explained: A Look at the Game and the Rules That Govern It*. New York, NY: Lyons Press, 1998.

Luxbacher, Joseph A. *Soccer: Steps to Success*. Champaign, IL: Human Kinetics, 2005.

Mielke, Danny. *Soccer Fundamentals: A Better Way to Learn the Basics*. Champaign, IL: Human Kinetics, 2003.

Radnedge, Keir. *The Complete Encyclopedia of Soccer*. London, UK: Carlton Books, 2000.

Skogvang, Bente, et al. *Soccer Today*. Stamford, CT: Thomson Learning, 1999.

BIBLIOGRAPHY

Brandbeat. "Soccer: A Global Game With National Appeal." March 10, 2005. Retrieved April 10, 2006 (http://www.brandbeat.com/brandbeat/?m=200503).

Crisfield, D. W. *The Complete Idiot's Guide to Soccer*. New York, NY: Alpha Books, 1999.

Decatur Sports. "U.S. Soccer Participation Steady at 18.2 Million." April 17, 1998. Retrieved April 7, 2006 (http://www.decatursports.com/articles/soccer_participation.htm).

Gifford, Clive. *Soccer: The Ultimate Guide to the Beautiful Game*. New York, NY: Kingfisher Publications, 2002.

Harvey, Gill, et al. *The Usborne Complete Soccer School*. London, UK: Usborne Publishing, 1998.

Ominsky, Dave, and P. J. Harari. *Soccer Made Simple: A Spectator's Guide*. Los Angeles, CA: First Base Sports, Inc., 1994.

Ramsay, Graham. *Soccer for Girls: An Introductory Step-by-Step Guide*. London, UK: Carlton Books, 1998.

INDEX

About the Author

Growing up in North Carolina, Brian Wingate spent many seasons on the soccer field. He played amateur soccer from age ten through high school. During his time at the University of North Carolina-Chapel Hill, Wingate played intramural collegiate soccer and coached a youth soccer team. Besides his playing experience, Wingate has served as a youth league referee.

Photo Credits

Cover (top, left), pp. 13, 16, 20, 21(bottom), 33, 36 by Darryl Bautista © The Rosen Publishing Group and Darryl Bautista; cover (right), pp. 1 (right), 18, 22, 26, 27, 30, 31, 34, 35 © Shutterstock; cover (field), p. 14 (bottom) © David Madison/Corbis; p. 1 (left) © Shaun Botterill/Getty Images; p. 3 (cards) © www.istockphoto.com/ozdigital; p. 3 (ball) www.istockphoto.com/Pekka Jaakkola; p. 4 © Bettmann/ Corbis; p. 6 Scala/Art Resource, NY; pp. 8, 10 © Getty Images; p. 9 © AP/ Wide World Photos; pp. 12, 17, 24 © www.istockphoto.com/Kirk Strickland; p. 19 © www.istockphoto.com/Dennys Bisogno; p. 21 (top) © www.istockphoto.com/Jordan Shaw; p. 29 © Joe McBride/Corbis; p. 32 © www.istockphoto.com/Mark Gilder; p. 37 © www.istockphoto.com/Alberto Pomares; p. 40 © Kim Kulish/Corbis; back cover (soccer ball) © www.istockphoto.com/Pekka Jaakkola; back cover (paintball gear) © www.istockphoto.com/Jason Maehl; back cover (football helmet) © www.istockphoto.com/Stefan Klein; back cover (football) © www.istockphoto.com/Buz Zoller; back cover (baseball gear) © www.istock-photo.com/Charles Silvey; back cover (basketball) © www.istockphoto.com/Dusty Cline.

Designer: Nelson Sá; **Editor:** Christopher Roberts